THE
EMPIR
EXHIBITIO
·
FIFTY
YEARS ON

A Personal Reminiscence
by Alastair Borthwick

PRESS OFFICER FOR THE EMPIRE EXHIBITION

GLASGOW, MAY-OCTOBER 1938

———— · ————

With additional reminiscences from a few
of the Exhibition's thirteen million
visitors

———— · ————

BBC · MAINSTREAM

FOREWORD

Magnus Magnusson

Everyone else remembers the Glasgow Empire Exhibition of 1938 with exultant nostalgia. My own memory is of intense disappointment – because I wasn't allowed to go to it. The Exhibition was Glasgow; I was Edinburgh. And for well-brought-up, middle-class Edinburgh schoolboys of those far-off days, Glasgow was on another planet.

My parents went, though (with what misgivings I have no idea). They drove there early one morning in the faithful family Lanchester, and came back that evening positively transfixed with pleasure and exhaustion. They adored everything about it – the colour, the excitement, the milling crowds, the far-off pavilions, the roller coaster, and especially the Highland Clachan. They ignored the fact that it had rained all day. They talked of the huge Tower they had queued for ages to whizz up by lift, but didn't grudge a minute of the waiting-time. My parents had only arrived in Scotland from Iceland a few years previously; mother, who was a great believer in fairies and the Hidden Folk, thought it was everything that fairyland would be, while father, who was a fervent Nationalist by upbringing and inclination, thought it proved just what Scotland could do for itself if given half a chance.

And for me, Glasgow would never again be the Badlands of childish imaginings and Edinburgh prejudice. Glasgow really was No Mean City.

This, with hindsight, was the central achievement of the Empire Exhibition. It put Glasgow on the map as a great City of Empire. It showed that Glasgow could do it. The home pavilions and displays far outshone the imports from the Dominions and the Colonies; the whole Exhibition was infinitely better than the 1924 Empire Exhibition in Wembley. And the image of Glasgow as a city of mindless gang violence and depravity was triumphantly disproved by the impeccable behaviour of the enthusiastic crowds who packed the Exhibition in their daily scores of thousands. But just as important was the effect on Glasgow itself and its civic pride. Glasgow had been wallowing in the trough of Depression, its fabled heavy engineering skills idle and useless, its menfolk emasculated by the insult to their manhood that mass unemployment had delivered. No wonder the hard men had turned to private gang feuding to restore their pride in themselves!

Almost fifty years to the day after King George VI and the present Queen Mother opened the Glasgow Empire Exhibition in Bellahouston Park, Glasgow celebrates the launch of another great exhibition: the Glasgow Garden Festival. Statistically, it feels a smaller event. The area of the site is 120 acres, compared with Bellahouston's 175. The cost is £15m, compared with Bellahouston's £150m at today's prices (£11m then). The target for visitor-numbers this summer is 4 million, compared with the 13 million who attended the Empire Exhibition.

But it won't necessarily be any less of an occasion. Although nothing remains of the Glasgow Empire Exhibition in Bellahouston Park except for the Palace of Arts, it lives on as a potent part of Glasgow's folklore. Will the Glasgow Garden Festival do the same? That will be the real yardstick of success.

18
MONTHS
TO GO

———•———

The Empire Exhibition began in the mind of someone on the Scottish Development Council. No one remembers who he was, but the idea became generally accepted by the Council's members and in the early summer of 1936 they held a meeting to discuss it seriously. They decided that an international exhibition ought to be held in Glasgow in 1938, or at latest in 1939.

The Department of Overseas Trade told them flatly that this was impossible: there was a convention among the nations limiting the number of international shows and it was not the United Kingdom's turn until 1947. But, said the Department, had they thought of an Empire Exhibition? That was how they had got round the convention at Wembley in 1924, and there was no reason why it should not be done again. The Council liked this. They existed to encourage new industries and convince outsiders that it was worth while to invest in Scottish skills and manpower, and an Empire Exhibition would have the weight to bring in Sassenachs and foreigners to see for themselves. After a public meeting held in the Merchants' House in Glasgow on 5 October 1936 they set up a company to organise such a show and retired from the scene, leaving the new organisation to get on with it.

◆

"The Exhibition let people know that Scotland was a country and not a bit stuck on to the top of England. We were a country and we could organise a great event."

◆

Committees abounded, as they always do in exhibitions. Anyone in Scotland who was anyone, or believed himself or herself to be anyone, was on at least one. There were committees for catering, art, history, publicity and other subjects by the dozen and indeed

Detailed layout of Exhibition
Picture: The Earl of Elgin's collection

The site under construction
Picture: Courtesy of The Glasgow Herald *and* Evening Times

Mr Thomas Tait, the principal architect
Picture: Courtesy of The Glasgow Herald *and* Evening Times

Above: Statue in the Scottish Pavilion
Picture: Courtesy of The Glasgow Herald *and* Evening Times

by the score. The final tally was 70 separate and distinct committees. Common sense, however, prevailed. The 45-strong Council of Management, realising that 45 people could not possibly manage anything, delegated everything to an Administrative Committee of five members under the chairmanship of Cecil M. Weir. These six controlled the project.

I should explain that this account is written from the viewpoint of a youngster who held a minor post in the Exhibition (I was second-in-command of publicity and ran the Press Office) but my work brought me in contact with these people. I feel strongly that, able though they all were, Weir in particular should be better remembered than he is. We called him Wee Cecil, though not to his face. He was a small, neat man who never raised his voice, was invariably polite, and made time even for small fry like me. He was knighted during the run of the Exhibition, and deserved it. If a decision was needed, he was the man you went to.

The first step was to appoint a general manager. He arrived 18 days after the Merchants' House meeting. Captain S.J. Graham, was a big-boned determined man who knew about exhibitions and was loaned by the Department of Overseas Trade for the duration. Next they needed money. Graham said that unless they could raise £250,000 inside three months they might as well forget it. Since the Exhibition was a company limited by guarantee this meant promises of cash to that amount, to be used if there was a loss at the end of the day. They raised the money in four weeks and in the end had a total of £705,000. Glasgow was in the habit of making its exhibitions pay (the 1888 and 1901 shows had both shown a profit) and confidence was such that this slender foundation was made to support expenditure of £10 million without the banks turning a hair.

Next the Exhibition needed an architect. At this point it is worth considering the options open to him. The usual drill in major shows was, and still is, for the architect-in-chief to design the layout and then leave the exhibitors – nations, big companies or whatever – to do much as they like with their own pavilions. (My happiest memory of the Paris Exhibition in 1937 is of two gigantic statues on top of the Russian Pavilion shaking a hammer and a sickle in the face of the eagle roosting on the roof of the United States Pavilion across the way.) The method has the merit of variety and stimulates competition, but architecturally speaking the result is a mess. This was not the method used at Bellahouston.

◆

"We felt it put Scotland on the map. It helped take away the myths that Glasgow was just the world's worst."

◆

The chief architect, Thomas Smith Tait, was a small round-faced man in a black jacket and pinstripe trousers who looked like a pillar of the Establishment, which he was: he was busy building St. Andrew's House in Edinburgh and had designed the architectural features of the Sydney Harbour Bridge. He grasped immediately that two facts about Bellahouston mattered above all others. First, big exhibitions took four years to plan and build, and he had only one-and-a-half. And second, he had a wonderful site if he chose to use it properly.

Bellahouston Park was an oblong with a hill inside it. The hill was 170 feet high and formed a ridge running from one boundary of the oblong halfway to the opposite boundary. Level ground surrounded it on three sides. Most architects would have had their pavilions on the hill, climbing in a crescendo to the top. Tait, so legend goes, took one look at the ground-plan and drew three straight lines, one along the flat ground on one side of the hill, another parallel to it on the other side of the hill, and a slightly shorter one joining them at the western end. These, he said, would be the three main avenues. The hill would be sacrosanct. It would have a tower on top and almost nothing else.

From the practical point of view this gave him flat ground to build on instead of the sloping hillside with its civil engineering problems. Every ton of earth unshifted was time saved. Given a simple building system the

Postcard of Tait's Tower, the main landmark of the Exhibition and one of the most popular attractions

OBJECTS OF THE EXHIBITION

1

To illustrate the progress of the British Empire at home and overseas.

2

To show the resources and potentialities of the United Kingdom and the Empire Overseas to the new generations.

3

To stimulate Scottish work and production and to direct attention to Scotland's historical and scenic attractions.

4

To foster Empire trade and a closer friendship among the peoples of the British Commonwealth of Nations.

5

To emphasise to the world the peaceful aspirations of the peoples of the British Empire.

deadline could be met. From the aesthetic point of view the layout gave him elbow-room. He could build an exhibition that relied for its character on space and vistas instead of the usual international free-for-all. He could build, for the first time on any scale, an exhibition that was planned to be seen as a whole, that could use relatively simple buildings to create a unity. He stood the accepted norm on its head. Instead of possibly brilliant buildings adding up to nothing, Bellahouston was all character and let brilliance go hang. I remember the pavilions as fitting the landscape, not as being outstanding in themselves. Indeed some of them, especially those of the Dominions, were downright bad. Nor do I remember the exhibits inside any of them. I do remember the gaiety, the space, the clean look to it all.

With the main avenues fixed, Tait chose a building method that was cheap, fast, and easy to reverse when the show was over. Most of the buildings had a steel or wooden framework and then had light asbestos sheeting hung on them. He sketched in cascades and staircases falling down both sides of the hill from the tower, and then chose a team of architects to tackle the pavilions individually.

Meanwhile Graham had started to build up a staff to run the show – no easy task, for with Wembley 14 years in the past there were almost no experienced people available. Even inexperienced people thought twice about interrupting a career in order to take an exhibition job that at most would last only a year or so. To be available one had to be out of a job through bad luck or incompetence. Graham had an anxious time, but he was a good chooser. We were a strange lot, but we managed. There were in the end 876 of us, from administrators to turnstile men, firemen (there were 29 in the Exhibition brigade), mannequins, bath chair attendants (six chairs at half-a-crown an hour), maintenance men for the fountains, season ticket sellers, 62 litter-men and a team to hose the avenues, a specialist from Whitehall to deal with ceremonial, and many others. Throughout the 18 months that remained to us we gradually got down to the job.

FLAVOUR OF THE TIMES

The Scotland we inhabited in 1938 was very different from Scotland today. People were the same as they are and always will be, but the quality of life was not. The basic facts were that despite the new housing estates rising on the outskirts of the cities, by far the greater part of the urban population lived in houses built in Victorian times. The people who lived in these houses were not well paid. They had just come through the great slump and even then 1,870,000 were still unemployed in Britain when the Exhibition opened. The rest worked for an average weekly industrial wage of 69 shillings, which is £3.45 in today's money. Prices of course were also low (a loaf cost less than 2p and one men's outfitting chain was still calling itself The Fifty Shilling Tailors), but they were nothing like low enough to let people spend as they do today.

◆

"There was no work for anybody at that time. When you went to the Exhibition and saw the exhibits you couldn't help thinking what a terrible waste of good machinery and good tradesmen."

◆

The small things give the flavour of the times. For example there was so little money about, and selling or renting anything was so difficult, that you could often cajole your landlord into decorating a room or two of your house for you. No one had ever heard of a smokeless zone: while the Exhibition was being built there were times in central Glasgow when visibility was down to fifteen yards. Almost nobody wore a beard. Horses still pulled ploughs and we hanged people for murder. The railways,

Illustration for the Australian Pavilion from the official guide

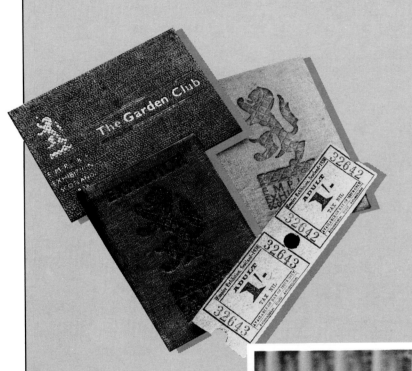

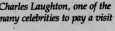

Charles Laughton, one of the many celebrities to pay a visit

Smile please . . . .

*Fifty Lister autotrucks scurried back and forth taking
people on short trips or sightseeing expeditions
Picture: Courtesy of* The Glasgow Herald *and*
Evening Times

unnationalised, had names –
London Midland & Scottish, for
example. Glasgow had two of
them, and four main stations. The
Herald and *Scotsman* had
advertisements on their front
pages. Letters had 1½d stamps on
them and postcards were a penny.
A semi-detached house,
brand-new, could be bought for
£650 or hire-purchased for 26
shillings a week. We read reports
of General Franco starting his
offensive in Catalonia, but paid
little attention to them. *The
Lambeth Walk* was two years old
but still being danced. Billy Butlin
had built his first holiday camp
and was starting another. In that
year the BBC, for the first time,
allowed programmes other than
news and church services to be
broadcast on Sunday mornings.
Cars were expensive (£250 for a
primitive family tourer was much
dearer in real terms than its
counterpart today) with the result
that the villages of Scotland, even
the most beautiful, were
uncorrupted by weekenders and
tourists. Smoking was a harmless
adult occupation, and youngsters
worked hard learning to enjoy it.
Cigarettes were cheap. They cost
6d for ten, and Woodbines 2d for
five.

◆

*"The Empire was important to us. We
always thought of ourselves as a very
large family and it was reassuring to
think that all these people were with us at
our time of need."*

◆

We went to theatres and music
halls (I can remember ten theatres
in Glasgow, and there may have
been more), but above all we went
to the cinema, queuing as a matter
of course in rain, frost or snow.
Programmes changed in mid-week
in the locals, and many people saw
both programmes. Nearly
everybody went once. One of the
definitive smells of the age was of
wet coats in the auditorium. The
cinema dominated our leisure in a
way that is unimaginable today. It
was not like watching television. It
was always an occasion. You had
to go *out* to the cinema.

Looking back it is astonishing to realise how law-abiding we were then – as the Exhibition itself was soon to demonstrate. It was not simply a matter of always finding public telephones in working order and not having to worry about bombs. It did not occur to most people, and especially the young, to misbehave. The Empire Exhibition had its own police station. It had one cell in it, and a force of 72 policemen and special constables. Out of the millions of people who attended during the six-month run they pulled in only 274, nearly all of them drunks. Crime barely existed. There was no vandalism at all. We were a biddable lot in those days.

◆

"We couldn't afford to go away on holiday so we bought a 5/- weekly ticket to the Exhibition. We went about three times a day."

◆

We were also a douce lot. Middle-class women, shopping in town in a heat wave, wore gloves and probably a coat as well. Their husbands went to work in lounge suits and, invariably, hats, and their only idea of leisure wear was grey flannels and a tweed jacket. Their shirts came with two collars for long wear, fixed on with studs fore and aft. Ordinary folk wore a suit and a cap, and my impression is that the women had a more restricted choice in the dresses they wore. Department stores and the rag trade were thriving, but the cheap end of the market did not have the variety it has today. And older women dressed older than they do now.

Business was picking up after the slump but only a few far-sighted people realised that we had only the threat of war to thank for it. In 1938 Britain built a third of all the world's ships and the noise of the rivetters was loud along Clydeside, but the writing was on the wall even then. In 1910 we had built two-thirds.

"I am sitting in the heart of the highlands on a wee brig writing this with all the thatched cottages around me . . ."

THE CLEUCH, DRYBURGH TWEED WAREHOUSE
EMPIRE EXHIBITION, SCOTLAND. 1938   X.145

A view from the Grand Staircase
Picture: Courtesy of The Glasgow Herald *and* Evening Times

But the clearest indication of the way we lived, and the way we thought of ourselves, lay in the houses we lived in, and especially in their contents. The slums were beginning to come down and new housing estates were transforming the outskirts of the cities, but there were 45,000 Scottish families still in homes officially unfit for

habitation. A corporation house was the first decent living quarters most people had ever had, but seen with today's eyes its contents were nearly always basic. It had a bathroom, a gas or electric cooker, possibly an immersion heater but more probably a coal fire with a back boiler. The tenants furnished it, bought a radio and linoleum for the floors (carpets were a luxury), and that was it. Hardly anyone had a refrigerator, deep freezes were unheard of, washing machines were only beginning to come into use, there were no television sets, and central heating was something that happened in America. But it was not the lack of these things that pointed to the way we saw ourselves. It was the fact that people could not conceive that they would *ever* have anything like that. To the working man and his wife in 1938 a piece of capital equipment as expensive as a refrigerator was utterly unthinkable.

◆

"The fact that it was raining all the time didn't affect the Glasgow people because it was always raining anyhow – it didn't make any difference."

◆

As to the look of our kitchens, fittings were of wood, including the draining-board which had to be scrubbed like everything else. There was no formica until the 1950s. The best we could do for work-surfaces was American-cloth.

There were no package tours either. So far as most of us were concerned, "abroad" had still to be invented.

POSTCARD MESSAGE

◆

"En route for a trip round this park on the miniature rly. Lunched opposite 'Atlantic' – not in it! Weather very showery and not good visibility so am waiting to go up Tower anr. day. Seen Princess Royal twice. Have 'done' some of the more important pavilions today . . ."

◆

The overwhelming fact of life was, of course, Hitler. He had been on the rampage from the mid-Thirties onwards and was clearly determined to have a war whatever anyone did to placate him. We lived from one broken promise to the next, and though it was obvious that time was running out we always hoped it would be better tomorrow. It is often said that the attendances at the Exhibition were affected by this. I doubt it. I was young and perhaps my elders, with one war already behind them, thought differently; but I know my generation did not bother its head with the threat of war. We did not want to believe facts so we did not believe them, and anyway there was no point in moping at home. We went out and enjoyed ourselves without any feeling of having a last fling. We knew and yet we refused to know. It was a curious time to live in.

Hitler walked into Austria while the Exhibition was being born. Until its end he dominated our world.

Picture: *Gordon M. Smith*

MODERN, SIMPLE AND SPACIOUS

*The Princesses inspecting the view
from the Tower
Picture: Courtesy of* The Scotsman

*Picture: The late Rev. George Allen's
collection*

The first object to appear above ground was the memorial stone unveiled by the King and Queen on 9 July 1937. The construction of the Exhibition proper took ten months, but months of planning preceded it. This was another strength of Tait's method. The hurly-burly of an international show always led to chopping and changing, second thoughts at the last minute, and general untidiness. With everything at Bellahouston under the control of a single team, jobs done once tended to remain done. The electricity supply, to take one important example, was all safely underground before building began, instead of trailing on poles to link up afterthoughts. Structural alterations did not bring demands for fresh coats of paint. When construction eventually began it was done in record time. No previous exhibition of its size had been built so quickly.

◆

"I can't forget the marvellous new style of architecture which was so different from the Leith tenements we were accustomed to. Everything was fresh, everything was clean and bright."

◆

The style Tait had decreed for the buildings was modern, simple and spacious, the standardised asbestos sheets giving huge flat areas which could be spray-painted. The colours varied according to the purpose of the building, and a good deal of nonsense was talked about symbolism. The Press Club where I worked was black and white, which was fair enough; but after half a century I still do not know why the Palace of Industry West was cream and red, and the Palace of Engineering silver and blue.

The public were even told that the inside of the Women's Pavilion was French grey because that was the most flattering colour for female complexions. No matter. The colours were splendid and they gave the Exhibition life.

Among the earliest works tackled were the excavation of a 400-foot lake on Dominions Avenue and the cascades which were to become one of the most effective features of the show. Starting near the base of the Tower on the hilltop they fell north and south to the main avenue, lit by underwater lamps and flanked by staircases. (The cost of running them, the lake and its huge fountain display, and the other fountains in the park turned out to be ludicrously small by today's standards. The electricity bill for the lot – pumps, lights, everything – was only £3,000, not per week but for the entire six months.)

The main pavilions followed, the building work being greatly helped by the weather, which throughout the spring was dry and sunny. There was a joiners' strike at one stage, and a fairly dotty dispute about the switchback in the Amusement Park, but in general the work went smoothly. The switchback affair is perhaps worth recording for its oddity value. The ride was a mile long and experts to assemble it quickly and safely could not be found in the U.K.. A German architect and four German joiners were brought in. The unions naturally insisted that they became members. This did not trouble the Germans in the least: they joined without demur, at which stage their Embassy intervened. It seemed the Nazi creed did not approve of trade unions. The men must resign. Graham had the makings of a first-class strike on his hands until it was explained to the Embassy that unions had two aspects, a pay-and-conditions aspect and a political aspect. Bellahouston had nothing to do with politics, and surely the Germans had no objection to having their pay safeguarded? Faces were saved and the strike was off. This nonsense cost the Amusement

◆

"I've been to Paris and all these places and I've never seen anything to impress me as much as the Empire Exhibition of 1938. I thought it was beautiful."

◆

The Butlin's Amusement Park
Picture: Courtesy of The Glasgow Herald *and* Evening Times

The United Kingdom Pavilion
Picture: The late Rev. George Allen's collection

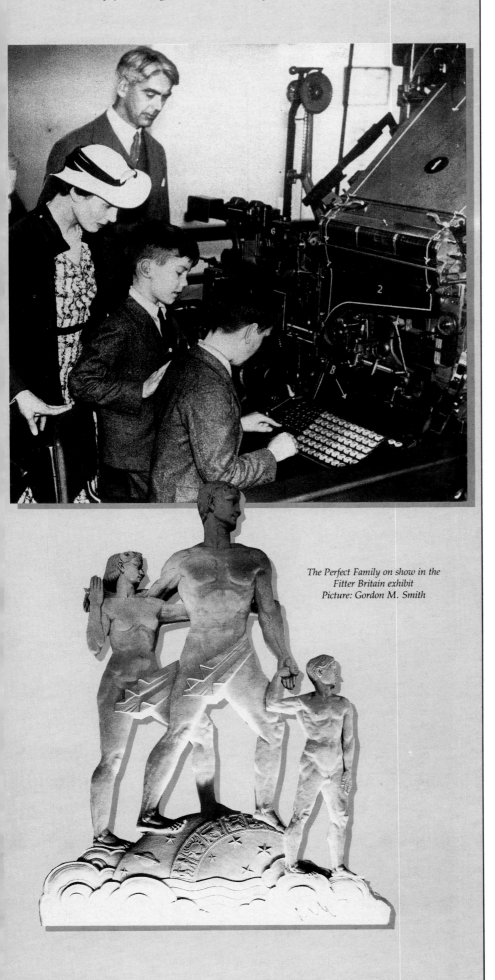

Trying out the Linotype in the George Outram's Pavilion
Picture: Courtesy of The Glasgow Herald *and* Evening Times

The Perfect Family on show in the
Fitter Britain exhibit
Picture: Gordon M. Smith

Park a week it could ill afford.

The memorable day for anyone involved in the Exhibition was not the opening day but the day before the opening. Three thousand men had been working for weeks to complete the show in time, and now they were joined by thousands more who were delivering the last-minute exhibits and bits and pieces they had been preparing outside. I left at midnight and there must have been at least 5,000 still hard at it. Policemen were on point duty wherever one avenue intersected another and the place was crammed with lorries. The pile of empty crates hidden behind the Palace of Industry West was twenty feet high. Everyone had his own crisis. I came back at eight next morning, and it was done. There were the odd things, but they did not show. Almost unique among major exhibitions, Bellahouston was ready on the day.

One of the most crucial anxieties of that last long day and night was the condition of the flowers, 10,000 pots each containing three tulips, buried in the flowerbeds. The glorious spring had been too much for them. They had been ominously full-blown when they were put into the beds a week before the opening, and sunny day had succeeded sunny day since then. By the night before the opening it was clear that they just would not do. They had to be taken out, 30,000 tulips down the drain, and (I think from memory) 10,000 hydrangeas were put in their place. There was further disaster to come. On the evening of the opening day the cleaning men hosed down the avenues and were not too careful about their aim. There was frost that night. After only one day on show the hydrangeas had to come out too.

Miniature Railway
Picture: Courtesy of The Glasgow Herald *and*
Evening Times

Many of the pavilions on Dominions Avenue were filled with goods for sale – mostly food, like grocers' shops
Picture: Gordon M. Smith

Interior of the North Scottish Pavilion
Picture: Gordon M. Smith

Picture: The late Rev. George Allen's collection

Picture: *Courtesy of* The Glasgow Herald *and* Evening Times

The golden days of radio. The BBC Pavilion displaying some of the stars of 1938 – Henry Hall, Bill Cotton, Sidney Lipton and Phyllis Robins
Picture: Gordon M. Smith

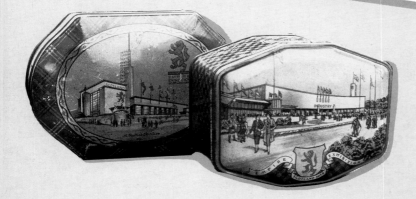

THE MAIN BUILD- INGS

The opening day, 3 May 1938, was all it should have been. The sun shone (though the wind was chilly), the flags flew, the fountains sparkled. The King and Queen performed the opening ceremony in Ibrox Stadium, then toured the Exhibition; and after the months of brouhaha the citizens were at last able to see what they had in their midst.

At one end of the lake stood the Palace of Engineering, at five acres much the biggest building in the Exhibition. It was popular, but it had had its problems and its exhibits were not so spectacular as they might have been. No railway line served Bellahouston and the park was surrounded by highways whose traffic flow could not be interrupted even temporarily, with the result that big exhibits such as locomotives could not be shown. However, anything up to 40 tons could be tackled and it is doubtful if the bigger items were ever missed.

◆

"I found the African pavilion interesting because at school we heard about these countries in our geography lessons but there were few pictures in schools in those days, and no films."

◆

At the opposite end of the lake was the Palace of Industry West, a huge bazaar holding almost every conceivable product except machinery. Along the two sides of the lake the Dominions and the Colonies faced each other. The Dominions, side by side along Dominions Avenue, had the prime site of the Exhibition and were intended to be its outstanding feature, but were in fact a fairly tatty collection, done on the cheap externally and filled with goods for sale, mostly food, like grocers' shops. Only South Africa grasped the opportunity, building a

Picture: The late Rev. George Allen's collection

Picture: Gordon M. Smith

The North Scottish Pavilion designed by Thomas Tait
Picture: Gordon M. Smith

Picture: Gordon M. Smith

pavilion in the form of a Cape Dutch house and using the interior for prestige rather than sales. The Colonies opposite mostly elected to share pavilions, but there were exceptions, notably the Burmese Pavilion.

"I thought it was marvellous – the pavilions, the giraffe-necked women, the Africans – and watching out for celebrities."

The transverse avenue linking the two main axes had Industry North, the United Kingdom Pavilion and the Concert Hall, and the northern avenue held the two Scottish Pavilions, one of which dealt with history and the other with modern achievement. Special mention must be made of the Women's Pavilion (its full title was The Women of the Empire Pavilion but nobody ever called it that), designed with a light touch by Margaret Brodie and vigorously organised by Lady Elgin and Mrs. Walter (now Baroness) Elliot. They wasted little time on static exhibits, though even when the displays were static they were good, notably the historical dresses. They received lady VIPs in a splendid reception room, and they had a fashion theatre that gave mannequin shows. The theatre was excellent, not only for its appearance but for the standard of the clothes it showed. The best fabrics Britain could provide were passed to the country's leading designers to do with as they pleased. A hundred thousand people paid to see them displayed.

In a corner of its own was the two-and-a-half-acre Highland Clachan, a hardy perennial (there had been a clachan, highly successful, in the Glasgow Exhibition of 1911) but admirably done, without excessive tartanry and with a regard for authenticity. There was a castle, an inn that served Scottish fare, a kirk, shops, a lochan, a burn, and three types of croft houses, one from Argyll, one from Skye and the third a round-ended black house from Lewis. They were a tremendous success, though general manager Graham, English by inclination if not by name, was none too sure of them. He wrote at the time: "While I have yet to be convinced of the desirability of displaying to the world at large, houses of the type in which no human being should be expected to live in the year 1938, there can be no doubt as to the drawing power of the Clachan." There was indeed no doubt. In the end 1,649,336 people paid to get in to it. Many even bought season tickets.

Special mention must also be made of the Palace of Art, designed and built to remain after

◆

"Some of the pavilions smelled really exotic – tea and incense. And there were beautiful men and women dressed in costumes displaying lovely carpets. It was like a fairytale."

◆

the rest of the Exhibition had been demolished, and still there in Bellahouston Park today. Collections public and private were scoured for the very best by Scottish artists. The result was memorable. It may not have been the most popular display in the Exhibition (though it did pull in half a million), but it was one of the best, possibly *the* best.

And there was the Tower, rising a sheer 300 feet from the hill, with galleries on top for 600 people at a time. The Exhibition catalogue said it was The Tower of the Empire, but nobody dreamed of calling it anything but Tait's Tower. The least believable statistic of the Exhibition was the figure for paid ascents. The Tower was served by two lifts, each holding eighteen people, not on the face of it a large capacity to cope with the queues that formed. In the event they hoisted visitors to the top, in bundles of eighteen, to the tune of an average 8,467 per *day*. There was always a queue. The final total was 1,312,392. The manufacturers claimed that no lifts had ever worked so hard.

◆

"The little buggies that ran about the Exhibition really intrigued us. Of course, wee boys kept jumping on and off without paying."

◆

The South African and Canadian Pavilions.
The former, built in dutch style, is now at an ICI site in Ayrshire
Picture: Courtesy of The Glasgow Herald *and* Evening Times

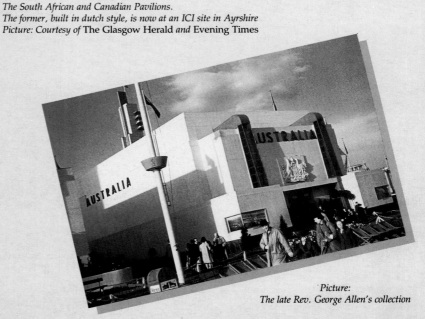

Picture:
The late Rev. George Allen's collection

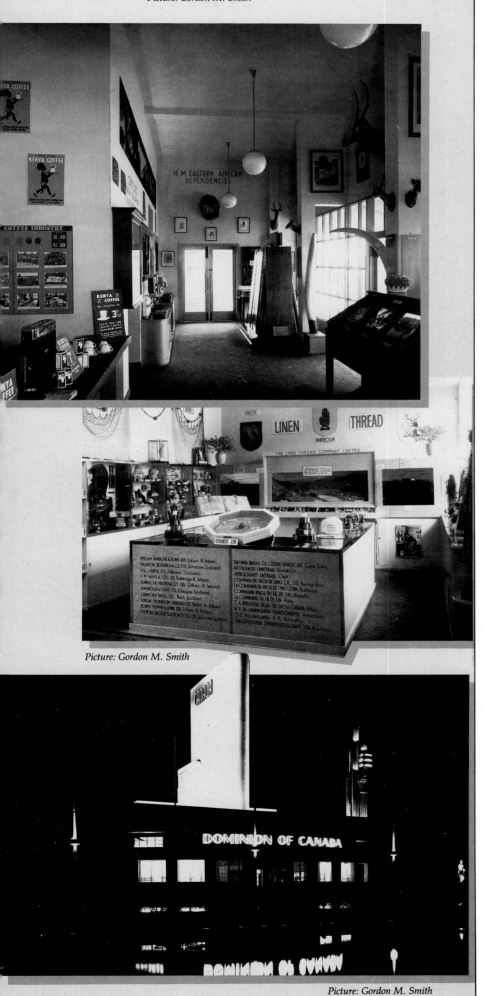

The Display Hall for the produce of East African countries. A nearby cinema showed films, some in colour, illustrating life in East Africa
Picture: Gordon M. Smith

Picture: Gordon M. Smith

Picture: Gordon M. Smith

These were the main buildings, but there were many others. The Garden Club (membership three guineas, later raised to five guineas) was possibly the most successful architecturally, and there was a Treetop Restaurant with trees growing up through the floor. The Atlantic Restaurant, high on the hill and shaped like the bows of a ship, was run by a shipping company and had waiters dressed as stewards. There were 62 private pavilions, put up by companies and various public bodies, and a large number of kiosks of standard, centrally-controlled design.

Transport was by little vehicles like motorised jaunting cars with the passengers sitting in two rows, back to back. Altogether they clocked up a million miles. And Billy Butlin ran the twelve-acre Amusement Park, the biggest in the country.

The Dominions and Colonies taking part in the Exhibition, either in shared pavilions or in pavilions of their own —

Canada, Australia, New Zealand, South Africa, Northern Ireland, Nigeria, Gold Coast, Sierra Leone, Burma, Kenya, Tanganyika, Uganda, Zanzibar, Malaya, Trinidad, Tobago, Jamaica, British Guiana, British North Borneo, Malta, Cyprus, Bechuanaland, St. Helena, Somaliland, Hong Kong, Ceylon and the Falkland Islands.

ONLY
THREE
DRY
SATUR-
DAYS

—————•—————

When the first few days were over
and people had found their way
about, several things became clear.
For one, the catering which had
been condemned as inadequate in
the early days, with queues
everywhere, sorted itself out:
visitors learned where all sixteen
of the restaurants were and did
not cram into some while others
stood empty. For another, the
places the public enjoyed most
were those where something was
happening, however simple. For
example, in a sea of machinery,
industrial goods and static
displays costing many millions of
pounds the Milk Marketing Board
had a little pavilion with twelve
cows in it and milked them
publicly three times a day. People
queued to see this amazing sight.
The milk sold, every drop of it, as
it left the udder. The Rhodesian
Pavilion had a much-advertised
water display simulating the

◆

*"I remember tasting real pineapple juice
for the first time in the Australian
Pavilion. What a difference from the
tinned pineapple syrup we got for Sunday
dessert."*

◆

Victoria Falls. It was well attended
despite the admission charge and
the fact that it was a fairly poor
show anyway. There was also the
case of Don Mundy from the
Australian Pavilion. One of the
many things Don, a cheerful
character, had done in his career
was sheep-shearing, and he issued
a challenge to anyone who cared to
try his hand against him. A
Scottish champion was found, and
when he was roundly beaten
complained that Don was using
electric shears whereas he was
accustomed to the old hand-
operated kind. Don picked up the

The Treetop Restaurant
Picture: Courtesy of The Glasgow Herald *and*
Evening Times

The millionth visitor at the Clachan
Picture: Courtesy of The Glasgow Herald *and* Evening Times

Crowds at the Paisley Road entrance
Picture: Courtesy of The Glasgow Herald and
Evening Times

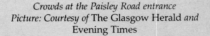

Women of the Empire illustration

Picture: Gordon M. Smith

old shears and beat him again. This competition, held on a platform by the lakeside, was possibly the most successful single exhibit of the entire show. The Clachan was another case in point. There were sheepdogs from time to time, and women carding wool, and tweed being woven, and the public loved them all. The big prestige displays were all very well, but there was no doubt at all about what went down best. I met a man the other day and reminisced with him. After fifty years the first thing he remembered was the cows.

◆

"There was a woman weaving wool and making stuff with wool and this was a thing we hadn't seen before – I didn't even know how wool was made."

◆

The earliest of the many events staged to keep the pot boiling was a football tournament in Ibrox Stadium with eight teams taking part – Chelsea, Brentford, Everton and Sunderland from England, and Rangers, Celtic, Aberdeen and Hearts from Scotland. Celtic won. There was a steady flow of celebrities throughout, mostly film stars, though the Aga Khan was among them. But the Exhibition provided its own momentum. Over 145,000 people flocked to see it on the opening day, 195,000 were there on the first Saturday, and from then onwards the popularity of the show was never in doubt in spite of everything the weather could do.

◆

"For me the novelty was the potato crisps. It was the first time I ever mind eating any. They cost 3½d a packet."

◆

The weather, it must be said, did a great deal. The dry spell which had helped so much during the months of preparation lasted only a week into the run of the Exhibition, and after that the heavens opened. Some said it was the worst summer for sixty years. Be that as it may, the Meteorological Office figures showed that 25.47 inches of rain fell during the six months compared with an average of 17.01

◆

– in other words, 50% more than usual – and to make matters worse a great many of the inches fell on Saturdays, when the best attendances of the week were hoped for. Only three Saturdays in the entire run were dry. Yet that was not the whole story. Freakishly, the sunshine figures were also up, not by very much, but nevertheless up. Bellahouston managed to average five hours of sun a day throughout the run. The weather was capricious and it was seldom possible to sit and listen to the bands in any kind of comfort, but my memories are of sunshine.

That said, the bad days were truly horrible, with the day of the Lord Mayor of London's visit one of the worst. I may be biased about this. I had a radio commentary to do. I stood on top of the Tower in a full gale and bucketing rain with a microphone in one hand and holding on to my top hat with the other: on State occasions we were very formal in those days. The greatest wet occasion of all was the night the Exhibition closed, but we shall come to that later. All in all the weather probably cost the Exhibition three million visitors.

THINGS OF INTEREST

Here are some of the things of "exceptional" interest listed in the official Exhibition guide.

AN EIGHTY-MILE VIEW OF THE COUNTRYSIDE and a panorama of the Exhibition: The Tower.

THE MECHANICAL MAN: United Kingdom Pavilion.

THE WORLD REVOLVING IN SPACE: United Kingdom Pavilion.

The Palace of Engineering
Picture: Gordon M. Smith

Lord Tweedsmuir, accompanied by Lord Elgin and Lady Aberdeen, adding a stone to the cairn beside the Peace Pavilion
Picture: Courtesy of **The Glasgow Herald** *and* **Evening Times**

One of the most popular attractions Picture: Gordon M. Smith

Picture: Courtesy of *The Glasgow Herald* *and* Evening Times

One of the croft houses in the Clachan
Picture: The late Rev. George Allen's collection

A BIRD'S EYE VIEW OF SCOTLAND: North Scottish Pavilion.

WOMEN'S FASHION FROM THE TIME OF GEORGE III TO THE PRESENT DAY: Women of the Empire Pavilion.

FARMHOUSE KITCHEN, where traditional Scottish dishes are cooked: Women of the Empire Pavilion.

MERINO AND OTHER FLEECES: Australia Pavilion.

MANUFACTURE OF POTSTILL WHISKEY: Ireland Pavilion.

VICTORIA FALLS IN REPLICA: Southern Rhodesia and East Africa Pavilion.

ASHANTI AND LOBI HANDICRAFTS: West Africa Pavilion, Gold Coast Section.

RUBBER ESTATE SCENE: Composite Colonial Pavilion, Malaya Section.

PINEAPPLE FACTORY SCENE: Composite Colonial Pavilion, Malaya Section.

"UNDER THE SEA" SCENE: Agriculture, Fisheries and Forestry Pavilion.

MYSTERIOUS DOOR, OPERATED BY INVISIBLE RAY: Palace of Engineering.

PUTTING THE EYES IN NEEDLES: Palace of Industry North.

WEAVING TARTAN ON A 200-YEARS-OLD LOOM: Palace of Industry North.

SPECIAL OCCASIONS

One problem in the early days was the Concert Hall, which was admirably suited to the purpose for which it was built, namely to house the best orchestras in the land. The acoustics were excellent, the seating comfortable. Unfortunately it was made to serve two purposes, not one. In the gaps between the prestige appearances (Sir Adrian Boult and the BBC Symphony Orchestra, Sir Henry Wood and the London Symphony Orchestra, Sir Thomas Beecham and the London Philharmonic Orchestra, a Kreisler recital, and a magnificent performance by Paul Robeson) bookings had been accepted from various choirs, most of them extremely local; and though the annual Mod could be relied upon to provide its own audiences, there were times when there were more singers on the platform than there were spectators in the seats. The Hall came near to being closed down altogether. Policy was, however, hastily overhauled, and Will Fyfe and other leading entertainers were summoned to put on variety shows, most of which were very good. They were more to Glasgow's taste than the choirs (and, to be truthful, Sir Thomas and his friends) and from then onwards the Concert Hall prospered.

Another relative failure in the

◆

"We never thought there was going to be a war tomorrow. The first time I realised it was really going to happen was when the management announced that our works was being altered so we could make bombs."

◆

early days was the Dance Hall, which was poorly attended except on Saturday nights. It was never a big draw. Much more successful was the open air dancing. The Exhibition was halfway through its run before anyone thought of this. It began when Jack Hylton and his band were playing in the Concert Hall (the best of the big bands all performed there – Henry Hall, Bert Ambrose, Roy Fox, Joe

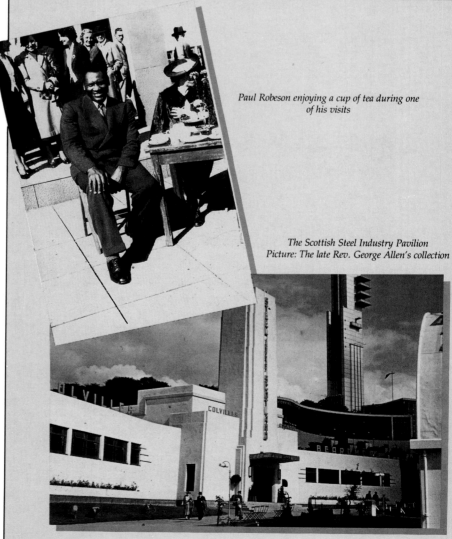

Paul Robeson enjoying a cup of tea during one of his visits

The Scottish Steel Industry Pavilion
Picture: The late Rev. George Allen's collection

Picture: Courtesy of The Glasgow Herald *and* Evening Times

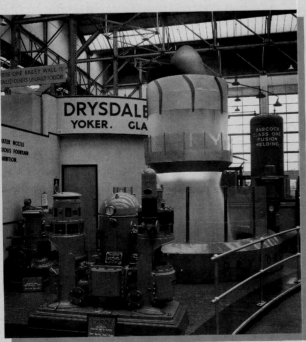

Picture: Gordon M. Smith

Loss and others) and he took his men along to the South Bandstand after the performance in the Hall was over. They played until midnight. From then onwards dancing was a regular and hugely popular entertainment, sometimes even in the rain.

◆

"I remember a war scare. The music that was playing all through the park was being stopped every few minutes and they were telling all the soldiers, and even the territorial army fellows, to report to the gate so they could be taken away in buses to their regiments. And wives, mothers and girlfriends were all crying and hurrying to the gates with their partners."

◆

There were Royal visits, not only on the opening day but at carefully spaced intervals throughout the run, and so far as the Exhibition staff was concerned they were fraught occasions. Field Marshall Montgomery once said he would sooner organise a battle than a Royal visit. We had seven – the King and Queen at the opening, the Duke and Duchess of Kent in June, and the Duke and Duchess of Gloucester in August, the Queen in September, and also in September three visits by Queen Mary. All of them were paced out beforehand and timed with stop-watches, planned in detail down to where each policeman would stand, and who would shake the Royal hand in what order, and many other things. The one that shook the people with the stop-watches most was the visit of the Duke and Duchess of Kent. The Duke was a bit of a lad. He side-tracked to the Amusement Park and we couldn't get him off the dodgems.

I remember, too, the King and Queen arriving in the U.K. Pavilion on the opening day. It had been arranged that the King was to "recognise" a sailor who had served with him at the Battle of Jutland. He headed towards the wrong man. The Queen Mum, then as now, had her wits very much about her. She dug him gently in the ribs, and all was well. It was beautifully done.

A different kind of occasion became popular with the public and was widely covered by the Press. This was the presentation of the freedom of the Exhibition to each millionth visitor and his wife or girl-friend. As the million mark was approached all the turnstiles were closed except two, one for the paying public and one for season ticket holders. They were carefully monitored, and when the lucky number came up a couple were pounced upon by Graham (or on the first occasion by Lord Elgin, the Exhibition president) and with the cameras clicking were given tickets for everything, including the best lunch or dinner the Exhibition could provide. The first winner was a Miss Isobel Duke, who was in the season ticket queue (where astute ticket-holders, realising what was happening, were dashing outside for a second shot) and was separated from her escort in the cash queue. He was reunited with her in a large crowd surrounded by policemen and thought she had been arrested. The unluckiest of those welcomed in this way was

◆

"I can't forget the crowds – the trams stopped every two or three minutes at the gates and the people were coming off and the trams went away empty. These trams held eighty or ninety people and they were all making their way to the Exhibition gates."

◆

the eight millionth visitor, who had a girl on his arm who was not his wife. His horror as the reporters and photographers converged remains a vivid memory. I squared the Press and we all went back and chose another eight millionth visitor, Mr. Arthur Watson of Glasgow, who so far as I am aware does not know to this day how lucky he was.

All summer the political situation was worsening, and in mid-September Chamberlain felt he had to report to the nation. I heard his broadcast in the Exhibition. The music from the loudspeakers stopped, and though there were thousands of people in the park there was silence, only the old man's voice and the sound of the fountains. Then the music came up again and we were back to believing what we wanted to believe.

Picture: Courtesy of The Glasgow Herald *and* Evening Times

Queen Mary was herself a popular attraction at the Exhibition. On the evening of her last visit there were 220,000 people in the park

The King and Queen on a tour of the Exhibition during the official opening, flanked by Sir Cecil Weir and Lord Elgin
Picture: The Earl of Elgin's Collection

PUTTING COLOUR IN THEIR LIVES

People have their own memories of Bellahouston in 1938. It was, after all, not a matter of exhibits but one of mood. You took your best girl there and strolled the avenues, took in the colour, danced at the South Bandstand, got a scream or two out of her on the switchback, enjoyed yourselves. There were, however, two outstanding occasions, certain to be remembered by anyone who took part in them. The first was the Saturday visit of Queen Mary on 10 September. She had come on the Tuesday, liked what she saw, and decided to come again next day. Still she had not seen enough and announced that she would come again on the Saturday. By far the biggest crowd the Exhibition had seen at that time turned out to greet her, 225,000 people packed almost immovably along the avenues, on the grass, over the flowerbeds, even up the trees. I had never seen anything like it. She was in a car with a string of other cars behind her carrying ladies in waiting, equerries, Exhibition notables and, right at the end, the Press who had been provided with cars because there was no other possible way for them to keep track of the proceedings. I was in the last car.

◆

"We used to get the tram to the Exhibition. That meant going through the Gallowgate. In those days it was a very drab, dark place so when you went through the park gates at Bellahouston it was like entering a different world."

◆

They were packed solid, a sea of happy people. They cheered the Queen, they cheered the notables, they cheered the Press, they

page twenty nine

cheered anything that moved. And there was this old lady, back like a ramrod, toque on top, not much given to smiling but smiling now. It took us a week to get the park back in shape.

Queen Mary sent a thank-you letter afterwards. She said it was the most memorable experience of her life, and as long as she lived she would remember with heart-felt gratitude the welcome given her. She had not thought it possible that a quarter of a million people could be so orderly. Well . . . thank-you letters are thank-you letters, but she did not need to go as far as that. I think she meant it.

The other great occasion, the final day of the Exhibition, was altogether memorable and at one time looked like being too memorable for comfort. Queen Mary had shown that very high attendances were possible, but the weather on 31 October was unpromising and it seemed unlikely that records would be broken. In the event they were, not only the Bellahouston record but the top attendance record for a single day at any exhibition ever held in Britain, Wembley included. The best Wembley could do in a day was 321,232. Despite rain which during the final stages became a continuous downpour, Bellahouston packed in 364,092.

No one who was there will ever forget it. By evening it was impossible to move freely: one simply went with the crowd. The peak was reached about 9 p.m., when the rain came down in earnest and people were still coming in while the faint-hearts had still not quite made up their minds to go home. The faint-hearts probably saved the day. Enough of them left to reduce the number of people in the park to about a quarter of a million, which was manageable, just. It had been intended that two pipe bands would lead everyone round the Exhibition for the last time, but mounted policemen could not get even one of the bands through. Dance music was played over the speakers, but dancing was impossible. Singing started at the South Bandstand and spread through the park, taken up by everyone, jam-packed with the rain beating down on them, and enjoying it. At 11.40 they sang *Auld Lang Syne*, liked it, and sang

Crowds queuing for entrance on the last day of the Exhibition. Many were turned away
Picture: Courtesy of The Glasgow Herald *and* Evening Times

it all again, facing inwards to the Tower which was floodlit by ten searchlights borrowed from the Services Pavilion. As midnight approached, a farewell message was spoken. ("I am the spirit of the Exhibition. I live tonight and die tonight. May memories of me abide in your hearts," and a good deal more in similar vein.) Then came Big Ben. The Exhibition flag

◆

"The Exhibition had given us all a lift. Then we were in the middle of a nightmare – worried about black-outs and rationing."

◆

was hauled slowly down, not without difficulty for the wind was blustery, and as it disappeared the searchlights snapped out. It was all over: and so though we did not know it was the British Empire.

The attendance for the six-month run was 12,882,548, and that in spite of the fact that it was never open on a Sunday.

The aftermath was relatively short. There was the usual public demand for the Exhibition buildings to be retained, but a clean sweep was made. The Tower, which for a time had several Clyde resorts competing for it, was broken up for scrap. The Palace of Engineering went to Prestwick, where aeroplanes are still serviced in it. The Cape Dutch house became an ICI staff canteen in Ayrshire and is still known as Africa House. Butlin bought the Concert Hall and some of the fountains, and the rest went at knock-down prices. The Episcopal Church of Scotland Pavilion fetched £45. At the end of the day the Exhibition guarantors were called on for 3/6d in the pound.

Did the Empire Exhibition achieve its objectives? Hardly. Hitler saw to that. It was not given time to reap the long-term benefits to industry which were hoped for. The gainer was not industry but the man-in-the-street who walked the avenues, and saw the colours and the fountains, and enjoyed himself. The final night was proof of its success. Quarter of a million people stood in the downpour to say goodbye to it, and they would not have done that if they had not had an affection for it. It had put colour in their lives, and they were grateful.

Ten months later we were at war.

Crowds in the park on the final night singing
Auld Lang Syne
Picture: Courtesy of The Glasgow Herald *and*
Evening Times

The Palace of Engineering now used by British Aerospace at Prestwick. It is a huge building commanding a five-acre site

THANKS FOR THE MEMORY

TWENTY HITS OF 1937-38
FOLKS WHO LIVE ON THE HILL
I'VE GOT MY LOVE TO KEEP ME WARM
SAIL ALONG SILVERY MOON
SOMEDAY MY PRINCE WILL COME
LAMBETH WALK
ME AND MY GIRL
HORSEY HORSEY
IN THE STILL OF THE NIGHT
THE LITTLE DRUMMER BOY
COME IN THE ALICE BLUE GOWN
DON'T EVER CHANGE
I CAN DREAM CAN'T I
DONKEY SERENADE
LITTLE OLD LADY
A TISKET A TASKET
I'LL BE SEEING YOU
JEEPERS CREEPERS
MY HEART BELONGS TO DADDY
YOU MUST HAVE BEEN A BEAUTIFUL BABY
TWO SLEEPY PEOPLE

SOME VISITING CELEBRITIES

EDDIE CANTOR,
PAUL ROBESON,
GRACIE FIELDS,
CHARLES LAUGHTON,
EDWARD EVERETT HORTON,
ELSA LANCHESTER,
MARGARET LOCKWOOD,
ANNA NEAGLE,
JESSIE MATTHEWS.

FURTHER READING

Neil Baxter, "1938" in *Glasgow's Great Exhibitions* by Perilla Kinchin and Juliet Kinchin, 1988.
Rudolph Kenna, *Scotland in the Thirties*, 1987.
Charles McKean, *The Scottish Thirties*, 1987.
C.A. Oakley, *The Second City*, 1975.